WONDERFUL WORDS

DOVER PUBLICATIONS, INC.
MINEOLA, NEW YORK

education.com

Copyright

Copyright © 2008, 2009, 2012, 2013, 2015 by Education.com
All rights reserved.

Bibliographical Note

Wonderful Words, first published by Dover Publications, Inc., in 2015, contains pages from the following online workbooks published by Education.com: *Spelling Patterns: Endings, Prefixes and Suffixes, Vocabulary in Focus, Stu-pen-dous Syllables,* and *Phonics Fun: Vowels and Diphthongs.*

International Standard Book Number

ISBN-13: 978-0-486-80262-6
ISBN-10: 0-486-80262-0

Manufactured in the United States by Courier Corporation
80262001   2015
www.doverpublications.com

CONTENTS

Spelling Patterns: Endings

Singular vs. Plural

A **singular** noun is an individual person, place or thing. A **plural** noun is the word for more than one.

Singular Noun	Plural Noun
cat	cats
house	houses
box	boxes
witch	witches

We add **s** and **es** to the end of singular nouns to show that they are plural.

Spelling Rules: Adding S to Make a Plural

For many words all you need to do is add an s to the end of the word. Examples:

cat ⟶ cats
egg ⟶ eggs
jump ⟶ jumps

There are exceptions to this rule. Use this chart to help you remember what to do to make certain words plural.

If the word ends in:	do this:	and add:	Examples:
-ch -s -sh -x -z	change nothing	-es	church ⟶ churches mass ⟶ masses brush ⟶ brushes match ⟶ matches box ⟶ boxes
consonant + y	remove the y	-ies	spy ⟶ spies baby ⟶ babies try ⟶ tries

How to Make a Noun Plural

Most singular nouns can be made plural by just adding an **s** to the end. For nouns ending in **x**, **z**, **s**, **sh** and **ch** you can form the plural by adding an es to the end.

Directions: Look at the pictures and write each noun in singular and plural form.

Word Bank

witch

airplane

box

book

sock

horse

lemon

Singular	Plural

More Than One

Write the plural for each word by adding **s** or **es**.

 apple _____

 fox _____

 brush _____

 ball _____

 tent _____

 sandwich _____

 watch _____

 ax _____

 pig _____

 house _____

 bee _____

 tomato _____

For words that end in **o** you normally just add **s** to make it plural, but there are exceptions.

Example: volcano ⟶ volcanoes.

Add **es** to these words ending with **o**.

 tomato _____

 potato _____

Plurals Word Search

Directions: Write the plural for each word by adding **s** or **es** to the end. Circle the plural forms in the word search.

 pencil _____

 cup _____

 fox _____

 crayon _____

 house _____

 cat _____

 witch _____

 box _____

B	O	X	E	S	B	R	Y
C	W	I	T	C	H	E	S
R	I	X	E	S	Q	C	G
A	J	C	U	P	S	A	F
Y	M	U	Z	O	E	T	O
O	O	P	E	S	A	S	X
N	H	O	U	S	E	S	E
S	P	E	N	C	I	L	S

Ends in y

For words where **y** follows a vowel, add **s**.
For words where **y** follows a consonant, drop the **y** and add **ies**.

berry _____

baby _____

bunny _____

boy _____

key _____

fly _____

spy _____

monkey _____

tray _____

toy _____

The Irregular Plural Noun

Make the nouns below plural but, be careful, they are irregular. Regular plural nouns just have an **s** at the end, but irregular plural nouns are different.

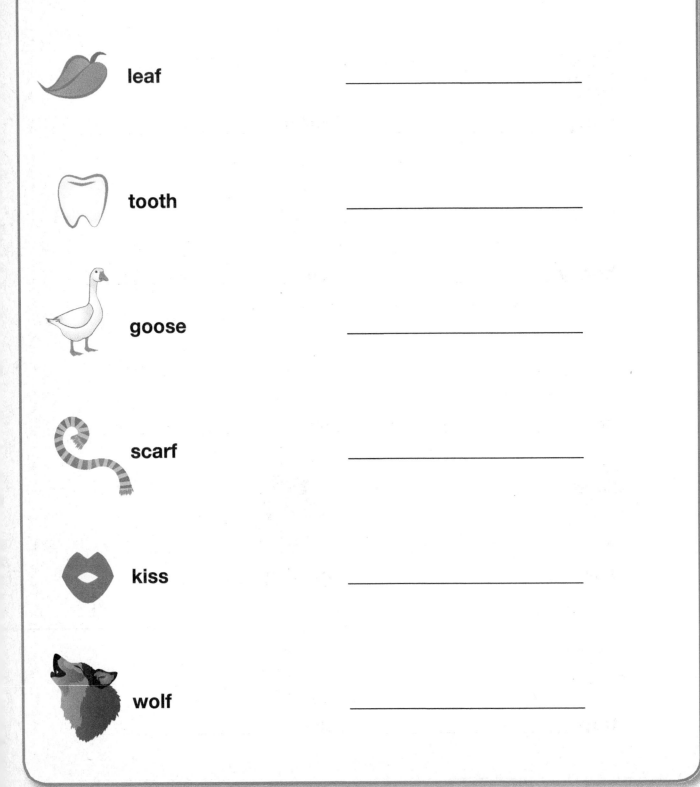

leaf
_____

tooth
_____

goose
_____

scarf
_____

kiss
_____

wolf
_____

More Irregular Plural Nouns

Make the nouns below plural but, be careful, they are irregular. Regular plural nouns just have an **s** at the end, but irregular plural nouns are different.

child _____

person _____

foot _____

ox _____

woman _____

fish _____

Verb Review

Remember that a noun is a person, place, or thing. Verbs are often used in sentences right next to nouns. In your own words, describe what a verb is.

_____

_____

_____

What are verbs that you've heard before? Write them here.

_____   _____

_____   _____

_____   _____

_____   _____

_____   _____

_____

_____

_____

Basic Past Tense

We add **ed** to the end of regular verbs to show that something happened in the past.

Directions: Read the first sentence, and circle the verbs. Rewrite the verb from the word bank into the second sentence to show that the action happened in the past.

Example: The children play at recess time.

Yesterday, the children ___played___ at recess time.

Word Bank				
ask	chase	depend	hand	walk

1. We depend on the car to get from home to school.

We _____ on the car to get from home to school, but now we ride the bus to school.

2. "Hand your homework in," said the teacher to her students.

The students _____ in their homework to the teacher.

3. I chase the ball across the field.

I _____ the ball across the field.

4. Did you ask to go to the park?

Yes, I _____ to go to the park.

5. Let's walk around the lake.

We _____ around the lake.

Double the Consonant

For some verbs, you need to double the last letter before adding ed. These words have a special pattern. The last three letters of the word have the pattern consonant-vowel consonant.

Directions: Change each word to the past tense by doubling the last consonant and adding ed. Then, draw a picture to illustrate the past tense verb.

Example: **nod**   _____nodded_____

stop _____

hop _____

skip _____

sob _____

Verbs that End in e

When a verb ends in **e** add only a **d** to the word to make it past tense.

Directions: Rewrite the words below to put them in the past tense. Then, find each word in the word search.

Example: dance ____danced____

smile _____

pick _____

pinch _____

sneeze _____

race _____

paint _____

rain _____

help _____

P	A	I	N	T	E	D	S
I	S	M	I	L	E	D	N
N	A	E	D	E	P	R	E
C	T	K	O	Q	D	A	E
H	V	X	C	B	U	I	Z
E	R	A	C	E	D	N	E
D	X	H	E	L	P	E	D
P	I	C	K	E	D	D	J

Verbs that End in y

When a verb ends with a **y** nd there is a consonant before it, the **y** changes to **i** before adding **ed.** Rewrite the words below to put them in the past tense. Then, find each word in the word search.

Example: study ⟶ studi + ed ⟶ studied

cry _____

try_____

fry _____

worry _____

hurry _____

carry _____

copy _____

dry_____

B	T	A	R	F	W	C	X
C	R	I	E	D	O	A	H
O	I	A	B	H	R	R	U
P	E	I	S	Q	R	R	R
I	D	P	R	B	I	I	R
E	H	Y	I	P	E	E	I
D	R	I	E	D	D	D	E
F	R	I	E	D	I	E	D

The Sounds ed Can Make

Adding **ed** to the end of a word can make three different sounds. Depending on the word you add **ed** to, it can sound like **"id," "d,"** or **"t."**

Read each word at the bottom of the page aloud, then write it in the correct column. Each column starts with an example.

"id"	"d"	"t"
batted	played	blinked

exited	bloomed	loved
agreed	dumped	smiled
added	baked	talked

Spot the Ending

Directions: Circle the correct past tense verb.

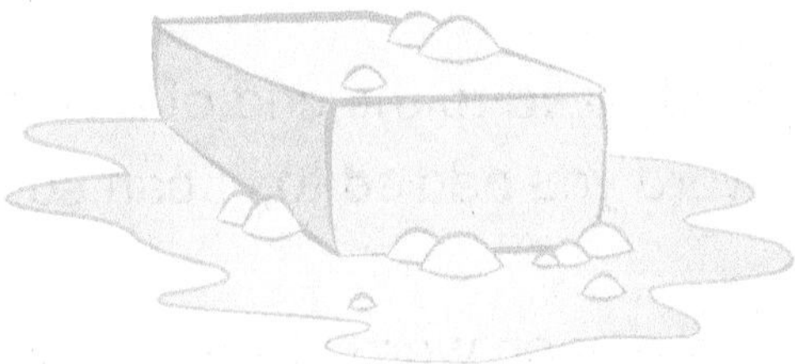

Example: bake

bakked   (baked)   bakd

wash	wasshed	washd	washed
relax	relaxd	relaxed	relaxxed
clean	cleaned	cleanned	cleand
smile	smilled	smild	smiled
visit	visits	visited	visitted
invite	invites	invitedd	invited
call	calld	caled	called
pry	pried	pryed	pryedd
live	livd	lived	livved
spy	spiedd	spide	spied

Verbs with ing

Rewrite each verb to tell what is happening now.

1. Are you _____ to open the door?
   (try)

2. He is _____ basketball with his friends.
   (play)

3. She is _____ a cake for the party.
   (bake)

4. We are _____ to music.
   (listen)

5. Tim is _____ his bike to school.
   (ride)

6. Sara is _____ for a book to read.
   (look)

7. Our school is _____ paper and plastic.
   (recycle)

8. I am _____ the cat.
   (feed)

Double the Consonant First

For some verbs, you need to double the last letter before adding **ing**. These words have a special pattern. The last three letters have the pattern consonant-vowel-consonant.

Directions: Change each word to the present tense by doubling the last consonant and adding **ing**. Then, draw a picture to illustrate the present tense verb.

Example: run   running
                        _____

tap_____   swim_____

pop _____   sip _____

Take Away the e

If the verb ends in a **consonant + e**, take away the **e** before adding **ing** to show the action is happening now.

Directions: Read the first sentence, and circle the verb. Rewrite the verb in the second sentence to show that the action is happening now. Remember to drop the **e**.

Example: I will phone my friends to invite them to my party.
I am   ___phoning___   my friends to invite them to my party.

Word Bank

dance	make	bake	phone	take	wake	smile	bite

1. I will dance when I hear my favorite song.

I am _____ to my favorite song.

2. We will make a card for our mom's birthday.

We are _____ a card for our mom's birthday.

3. Do you want to bake cookies or a cake?

We are _____ brownies!

4. He will have to wake up early for the trip.

He is _____ up.

5. Try to smile for the picture.

Everyone is _____ for the class picture.

6. Dad will take us to the zoo.

Dad is _____ us to the zoo right now.

Change ie to y Before Adding ing

If the verb ends in an **ie** change the **ie** to **y**. Then add **ing** to show the action is happening now. Rewrite the words below, then find each word in the word search.

die _____

lie _____

tie _____

vie _____

I	T	A	V	Y	I	N	G
F	R	T	Y	I	N	G	R
I	D	K	X	R	S	H	E
G	Y	L	H	M	E	R	W
N	I	N	A	Y	G	E	J
T	N	G	D	Z	W	T	U
R	G	A	R	Q	R	R	N
B	A	L	Y	I	N	G	G

Consonant Endings: ed and ing

For each list circle the correct –ed and –ing ending for the verb.

walk	walkked	(walked)	(walking)	wakking
jump	jumped	jumpped	jumpping	jumping
slap	slapped	slaping	slapping	slaped
pin	pinned	pinning	pined	pineng
dot	doted	dotted	doting	dotting
tan	tanned	taning	taned	tanning
wag	wagdd	wagged	waggeng	wagging
wink	winkdd	winked	winking	winkking
tug	tuging	tuged	tugging	tugged
pull	puling	pulled	pulling	puled

Write the correct **ed** or **ing** endings for the word given.

1. Frank (tap) _____ his foot to the music.

2. Kristi is (put) _____ the cake in the oven.

3. Mindy (play) _____ with her friends after school.

4. Mark is (look) _____ for his other sock.

An End

Rewrite each word with the correct form of the ending **ed.**

wish _____   cry _____

stop _____   cough _____

hurry _____   sneeze _____

laugh _____   pop _____

nod _____   time _____

Complete each sentence with the correct word from the box. Spell the word correctly with **ing** at the end.

Word Bank					
worry	bob	wave	take	smell	keep

1. At the Halloween party we are _____ for apples.

2. He is _____about the math test this week.

3. She is _____at the animals at the zoo.

4. They are _____their house clean by sweeping every day.

5. Mike does not like _____the trash out.

6. Mom was _____the flowers at the park.

Great job!

_____

is an Education.com writing superstar

Prefixes and Suffixes

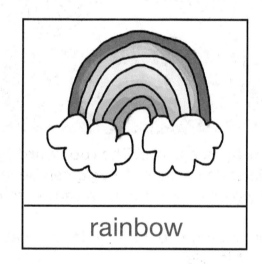

rainbow

WHAT IS A *PREFIX*?

A **prefix** is attached at the *beginning* of a word and *changes* that word's **original definition.**

prefix   root word

The **prefix _bi_** means *two*. The **root word _cycle_** has a lot of different meanings. A **_cycle_** can be *many events grouped together*, or it can be a verb — *to move.*

When you put together **bi + cycle,** you get a totally new word: **bicycle!**

Night	Candle	Drive	Tour
Untie	Lit	Return	Run
Order	Mistake	Turn	Reverse

Circle all of the words above that have prefixes.

WHAT IS A <u>SUFFIX</u>?

A **suffix** is a letter or a group of letters placed at the
end **of a word** to *change* the word's **meaning.**

DUCK LING
root word   suffix

The **suffix** *<u>ling</u>* means *belonging to a group.* The
root word *<u>duck</u>* is the name of a *quacking, fluffy bird.*

When you put together **duck + ling,** you get a baby
bird: a **duckling!**

Pig	Drive	Act	Careful
Piglet	Teach	Painless	Night
Actor	Darkness	Care	Untie

Circle all of the words above that have suffixes.

COMPOUND WORDS

By joining two smaller words together to make one new word, you create a **compound word**. For example, the word *rainbow* is a **compound word** because you combine the words *rain* and *bow*.

Take apart each compound word, making two smaller words. Draw a picture in the boxes for each smaller word.

Example:

1. rainbow

rain + bow = rainbow

2. jellyfish

+ =

3. butterflies

+ =

WRITE COMPARING WORDS

Look at the block pyramids below. The word in each top block is a root word. In the middle block, add —*er* to the base word by writing the word. In the bottom block, add —*est* to the base word. Write each word out.

Example

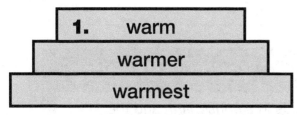

1. warm
warmer
warmest

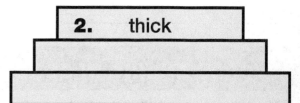

2. thick

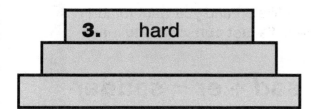

3. hard

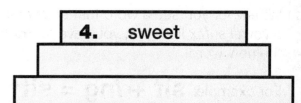

4. sweet

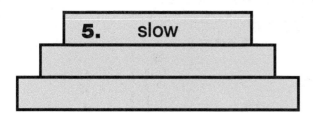

5. slow

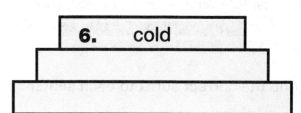

6. cold

Now write a sentence using at least one of the words you wrote.

_____

_____

_____

VOWEL & CONSONANT SUFFIXES

Just like there are vowel and consonant words, there are also **vowel suffixes** and **consonant suffixes**.

A **vowel suffix** begins with a vowel: -able, -er, -ed, -ing, -ity, -ation, -est, -al, -y

A **consonant suffix** begins with a consonant: -ship, -less, -some, -ful, -hood, -let,
-less, -ment

WORDS ENDING IN CONSONANTS + VOWEL SUFFIXES

How do you spell sit + -ing? The root word **sit** ends in a *consonant*, and the suffix **-ing** starts with a *vowel*. Something special happens!

Whenever you see a word that *ends in a consonant* like **sit** and you want to add a *vowel suffix* like **-ing**, you have to **double the word's last consonant** to make the new word!

For example: **si*t* + *i*ng = sit̲ting   sa*d* + er = sadd̲er**

Exceptions: This rule doesn't work for root words that end in w, x, or y.
Example: snow + ed = snowed, play + ed = played, box + ed = boxed.

Add the correct suffix to each sentence. The first is done for you.

1. The cat ____*begged*____ for the mouse toy. (*ed,* *er*)
beg

2. Aunt Dottie _____ at the red light. (*ed, ing*)
stop

3. I enjoy _____ by the fire. (*able, ing*)
sit

4. My friends _____ the balloon. (*ed, er*)
pop

5. The dalmatian is very _____. (*y, ing*)
spot

30

VOWEL & CONSONANT SUFFIXES

WORDS ENDING IN CONSONANTS + CONSONANT SUFFIXES

If the word ends in a consonant (*spot*) and you add a suffix that begins with a consonant (-*less*), then there are no spelling changes (**spotless**).

For example: **sad + ly = sadly   mad + ness = madness**

WORDS THAT END WITH "Y" OR "OW" + SUFFIX "ER" OR "EST"

How do you spell happy + -est? The root word **happy** ends in "y." So in special cases like these, you turn the "y" into an "i" when you add the suffix "er" or "est."

For example: **happy + est = happiest**

Add the correct suffix to each sentence. The first is done for you.

1. My sister's room is very tidy and ____*spotless*____. ((less) ly)
   spot

2. Which is _____, gummy bears or popcorn? (er, est)
   tasty

3. Jeremy _____ at the store for a new tie. (s, ly)
   shop

4. I _____ ate the candy apple. (ness, ly)
   glad

5. Gina _____ the collar over the dog's head. (s, ly)
   slip

6. My brother is _____ than I am. (er, est)
   sloppy

7. I love running and _____. (y, ness)
   fit

8. John thinks clowns are the _____ people in the world. (er, est)
   funny

SPECIAL SUFFIX RULES

Now that you have a better understanding of what a suffix is, let's dive into some rules about suffixes and words.

Let's refresh what you've learned! Use the following as reference for future practice.

SUFFIX

A word ending that is attached to a root word, changing its meaning.

small + _er_ = smaller

VOWELS & CONSONANTS

Vowels include: **a e i o u**.
Sometimes **y** is considered a vowel.

Any letter that isn't a vowel is called a _consonant_.
b c d f g h, etc. are all consonants.

SYLLABLES

A way to break down a word based on rhythm. Try clapping your hands as you say a word, and count the claps. Each syllable will always have a vowel.

One-syllable words:
 dog, help, job, love
 cat, run, play

Two-syllable words:
 bunny, funny, daddy

Multiple-syllable words:
 understand, happily

Practice your understanding of suffixes, vowels & consonants, and syllables.

1. HAPPINESS

a) Write out the suffix: _____

b) Does the word start with a vowel or a consonant? _____

c) Break down the word into syllables: _____

2. UNDERSTANDING

a) Write out the suffix: _____

b) Does the word start with a vowel or a consonant? _____

c) Break down the word into syllables: _____

SUFFIX COMPARISONS

Use the following worksheet to illustrate –er and –est words.

Make comparing words that you'd like to show! Some great examples of comparing words are: tall, taller, tallest; small, smaller, smallest; or fast, faster, fastest.

Draw pictures in the blank boxes below to show the meaning of each word.

Be sure to write the word below each picture!

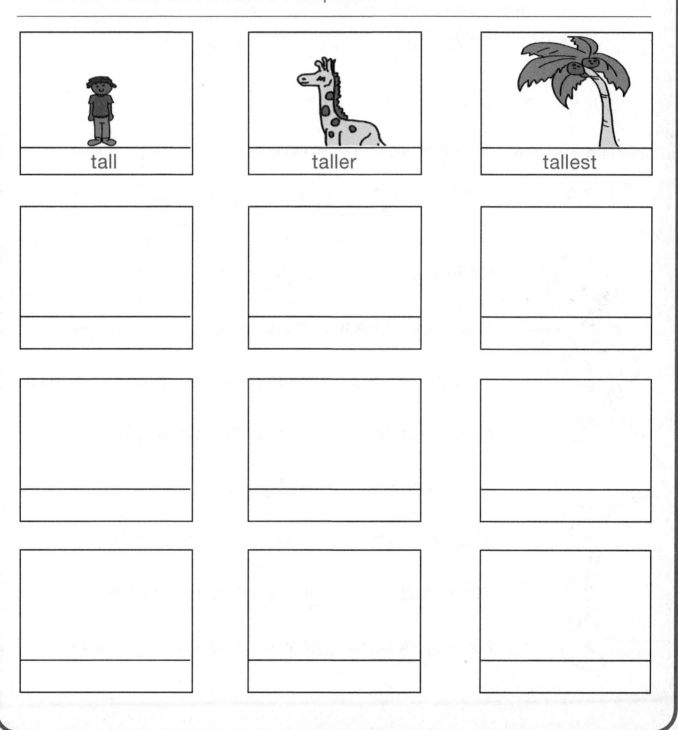

tall

taller

tallest

UN *prefix* **HAPPY** *root word* **REST** *root word* **LESS** *suffix*

Negative prefixes and suffixes alter the root word to mean "the opposite of," "not," or "against."

NEGATIVE NELLIE

Complete each word in the following sentences using a prefix or suffix from the word bank.

im **un** **anti** **less** **dis**

Nellie is a very ____happy person.

She's never pleased and is always ____appointed.

____patient and quick-tempered, she gets angry easily.

Nellie has many ____likes and enjoys very little.

Nellie is humor____ and grumpy.

She's incredibly ____polite to teachers and other adults.

She is care_____ with toys that don't belong to her.

Nellie dislikes many people and is very ____social.

Positive prefixes and suffixes help emphasize a root word's original meaning.

POSITIVE PETE

Complete each word in the following sentences using a prefix or suffix from the word bank.

ful   **over**   **pro**   **ish**

Pete is a very hope_____ and positive person.

His friends say he _____flows with happiness.

He is very _____active and always does the best thing.

Sometimes Pete is called child_____, but he's just playful.

Pete is rather clown_____ and loves to make others laugh.

He is very thought_____ and loves gift-giving.

Respect_____ and sweet, Pete has many good qualities.

MORE, MOST, AND SUFFIXES

TWO SYLLABLE ADJECTIVES + SUFFIX "FUL"

If an adjective has **2 syllables** (*color*) and also <u>ends</u> with the suffix *"ful"* (*colorful*), you need to add *"more"* or *"most"* before the word if you want to write **comparisons.**

For example: **color (col • or) + ful = colorful.**
Butterflies are *more colorful* than moths.

Complete each comparative sentence using the right word. The first is done for you.

1. I find my sister is way _____*more*_____ **cheerful** than my brother. (*more*, *most*)

2. Puppies are the _____ **playful** pets. (*more*, *most*)

3. Do you think elephants or sharks are _____ **powerful**? (*more*, *most*)

THREE (OR MORE) SYLLABLE WORDS WITH SUFFIXES

If an <u>adjective with a suffix</u> has *3 or more syllables*, always add *"more"* or *"most"* before the word when you write **comparisons**.

For example: **excite + ing = exciting (ex • cit • ing).**
Jon is the *most exciting* person I know.

Complete each comparative sentence using the right word.

1. Sometimes Joe can be _____ **talkative** outside of class. (*more*, *most*)

2. Cooks try to find the _____ meal **combinations**. (*more*, *most*)

3. Are monkeys _____ **entertaining** than cats? (*more*, *most*)

TESTING SUFFIX SKILLS

Now that you are familiar with vowel suffixes, consonant suffixes, comparisons, and how spellings can change, practice the following exercises!

Use the correct adjective for each sentence below. The first is done for you.

1. My cookie is ____*bigger*____ than my brother's, but our father chose the

____*biggest*____ cookie from the jar. (*big*)

2. The dog was _____ than the cat when you gave him a bone,

but he was the _____ when we played fetch with him. (*happy*)

3. I thought the kitten was _____ than the cat, but the puppy was

the _____ out of all the animals in the pet store. (*playful*)

4. John _____ picked the first ice cream scoop. (*glad*)

5. Which do you find _____, a monkey or a clown? (*funny*)

6. The movie made me _____ the more I watched it. (*sad*)

PRACTICE NUMBER PREFIXES

Use a dictionary to find out what each word means.
Fill in the blanks by drawing in a picture or writing out the word.

BI   +   **CYCLE**   =

3   +   **ANGLE**   =

     +   =   **UNICORN**

TRI   +   **POD**   =

MAKE NEW WORDS WITH SUFFIXES

Choose a root word that fits with the suffixes below. Write your root word in the first box. Combine it with the suffix and write the new word.

Root Words

color   chew   fair   treat   sad   like   help   silent

	Root Word	+	Suffix	=	New Word
1.	chew	+	-able	=	chewable
2.		+	-ful	=	
3.		+	-less	=	
4.		+	-able	=	
5.		+	-ly	=	
6.		+	-ness	=	
7.		+	-ful	=	
8.		+	-ly	=	

UNSCRAMBLING PREFIXES

Unscramble the words. Be sure to circle the word's prefix!

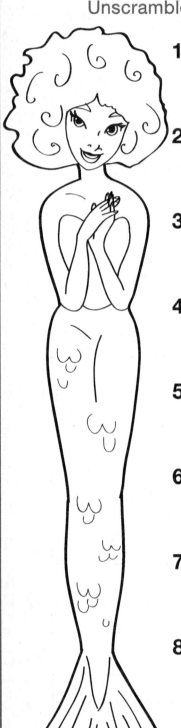

1. A creature that is half woman, half fish.

  eradmim: _____(MERMAID)_____

2. A tank where you can keep fish in your home.

  uaumqari: _____

3. An eight-legged sea animal.

  tusoopc: _____

4. These tools help you see things from far away.

  eepeltcos: _____

5. A bird that can be found by the ocean.

  lugasle: _____

6. Scientific study of animals.

  lozooyg: _____

7. A war ship that can dive underwater.

  suaienrmb: _____

8. Under the surface of the water.

  edawnerrut: _____

PREFIX SEARCH

Read the fable <u>The Crow and the Water Jug</u> below.
Circle all of the words that have prefixes in the story. *Clue: There are 5 words total.*

AN UNHAPPY CROW CHOKING with thirst saw a big clay jug, and hoping to find water, flew to it with delight. When he reached it, he sadly realized that it contained so little water that he could not possibly get at it.

He tried everything he could think of to reach the water, but all his efforts were in vain. Suddenly, the crow had an idea!

He flew away and returned with a stone, dropping it into the pitcher. The water raised a little, making room for the stone. Happy with his discovery, the crow collected as many stones as he could carry and dropped them one by one with his beak into the pitcher, until he brought the water within his reach and had a nice, refreshing drink!

Little by little does the trick.

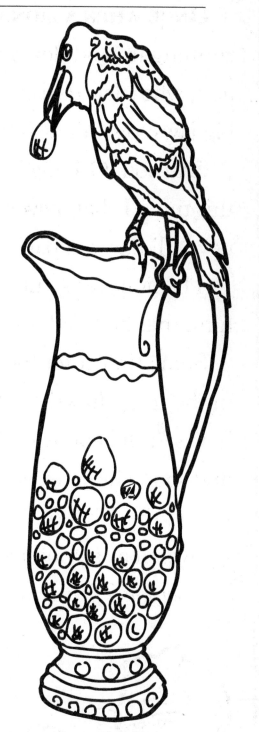

SUFFIX SEARCH

Read the fable <u>The Lion and the Mouse</u> below.
Circle at least 5 words that have suffixes in the story. *Clue: There are 13 words total.*

ONCE WHEN A LION was sleeping a little mouse began running up and down on top of him; this soon woke up the lion, who placed his huge paw on top of him, and opened his big jaws to swallow him.

"Pardon, O King," squeaked the little mouse: "forgive me this time, I shall never forget it: I promise if you let me go now, I'll pay you back!"

The lion was so tickled at the idea of the mouse helping him, that he lifted up his paw and let him go.

Some time after the lion was stuck in a rope trap dangling in the trees. Just then the little mouse walked by, and seeing how sad the lion was, went up to him and soon chewed away the ropes that bound the King of the Beasts, proving his worth as a good friend.

Even small friends are great friends.

BUILD A WALL

Build a wall by having an adult help you cut out all the pieces below. Connect the correct prefix or suffix to a word. Use the definitions below the unfinished words if you need help. Be sure to glue each prefix or suffix where it belongs!

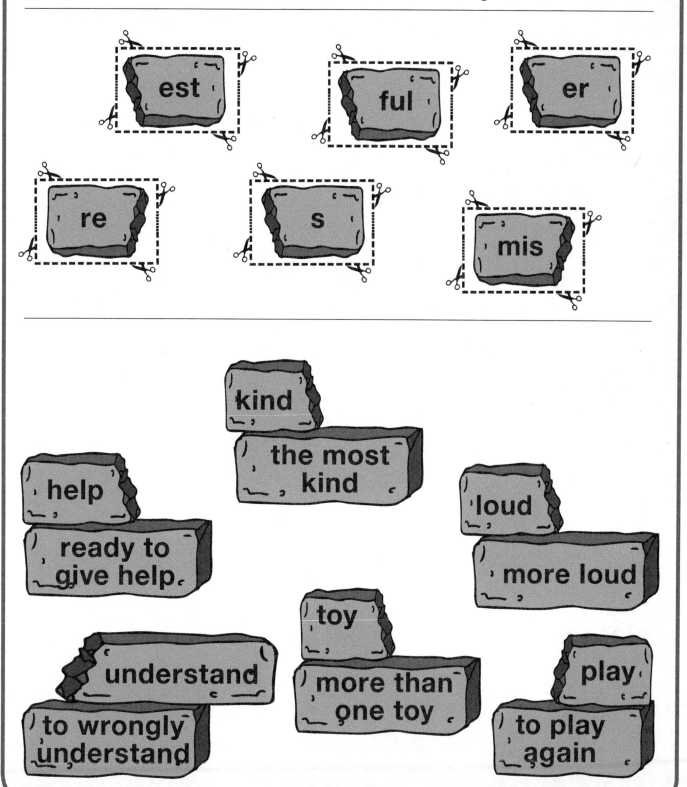

est

ful

er

re

s

mis

kind
the most kind

help
ready to give help.

loud
more loud

understand
to wrongly understand

toy
more than one toy

play
to play again

PREFIX CROSSWORD PUZZLE

There are many animals whose names start with prefixes!
Complete the following crossword puzzle and circle the
prefixes once you've filled out the puzzle.

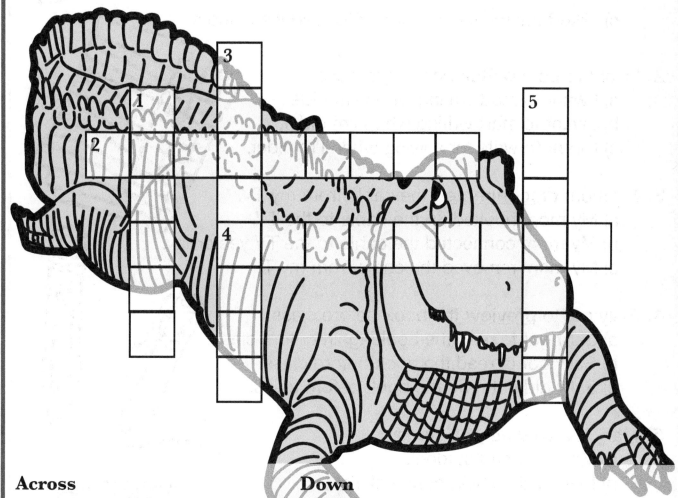

Across

2. An insect with hundreds of legs!
4. A reptile with big jaws.

Down

1. Another word for cat.
3. This animal has a long snout to suck up ants.
5. An eight-legged sea animal.

Word Bank

feline   anteater   alligator   centipede   octopus

PREFIX/SUFFIX MULTIPLE CHOICE

Circle the answer that best describes the meaning of the underlined word.

1. I loved the movie so much I had to **rewatch** it!
  a) I liked the move so much I watched it twice.
  b) I liked the movie so much I watched it again.
  c) I liked the movie so much I stopped watching it.

2. I want to be a **writer** when I grow up!
  a) I want to read writing when I'm older.
  b) I want to start writing when I'm older.
  c) I want to write for a living when I'm older.

3. My mom **disconnected** the cable from my TV.
  a) My mom hooked up the cable to the TV.
  b) My mom connected the cable to the TV yesterday.
  c) My mom removed the cable from my TV.

4. Sally got to **preview** the book before class.
  a) Sally got to read the book again before class.
  b) Sally got to read the book before class.
  c) Sally did not read the book before class.

5. Mary is a very **helpful** student.
  a) Mary is a bad student.
  b) Mary is little help during class.
  c) As a student, Mary helps a lot.

6. John **unwrapped** his present during the party.
  a) John hid his present during the party.
  b) John played with his present during the party.
  c) John opened his present during the party.

SUFFIX-PREFIX GAME

Now that you know about suffixes and prefixes, let's play a game!

1) Cut out the cards below. Be sure to have an adult supervise.

2) Find a couple of friends to play with.

3) Spread out the cards. Everyone will take turns making new words, starting with one card and adding one card per turn.

4) Be sure to look up your words in a dictionary to make sure they are real words.

5) The player who makes the most words wins the game!

cheer	pay	-less
kind	run	care
-ly	-ful	un-
care	wash	play
friend	sad	fear
-able	-ness	re-
tie	real	fair

Great job!

_____

is an Education.com reading superstar

Vocabulary in Focus

Same Sounds

Circle the correct **homophone** to complete the sentence.

Homophones are words that sound the same but have different spellings and meanings.

1. I just (eight / ate) a lot of (meat / meet) for dinner.

2. I can't (wait / weight) to receive your letter in the (male / mail)!

3. My mom bought (two / to) pounds of delicious (beats / beets).

4. Jack is spending the (weak / week) with his (aunt / ant).

5. We (won / one) (hour / our) first basketball game!

6. Would you like to (where / wear) a (pear / pair) of my mittens?

7. Mr. Smith's (son / sun) is an (I / eye) doctor.

8. (Their / There) is an (acts / ax) over by the tree.

Simone's Homophones

Simone is an excellent speller, but she tends to get confused when two words sound similar. Help Simone write what she means by underlining each incorrect homophone and writing the correct word on the lines given.

I walked inn to the pet store because their was a sign that said "Puppies for Sail." The cutest one had a short tail and white pause.

_____ _____ _____ _____

When I'm board and my mom isn't home, I like two try on her high healed shoes. There difficult to ware, but they make me three inches taller.

_____ _____ _____

My cousin Julius scent me a postcard in the male. He is at the beach in Hawaii with his knew surfboard. He has been surfing four over twenty years.

_____

_____

_____

_____

I can't weight for softball season this year. My too favorite positions to play are write field and third bass.

_____

_____

_____

Check the Homophones

Homophones are words that sound alike, but have different meanings.
The sentences below have the wrong homophones in them.
Circle the homophone and write the correct word in the space provided.

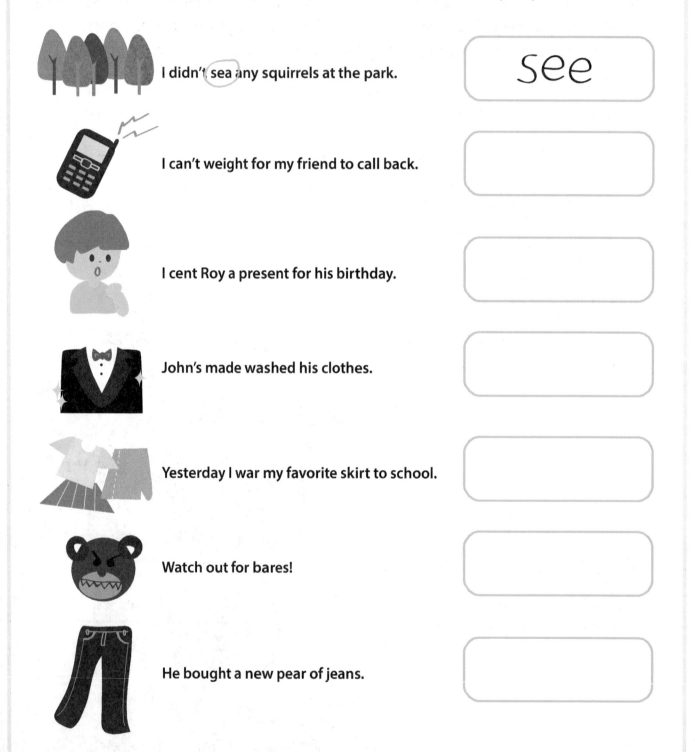

I didn't (sea) any squirrels at the park.

see

I can't weight for my friend to call back.

I cent Roy a present for his birthday.

John's made washed his clothes.

Yesterday I war my favorite skirt to school.

Watch out for bares!

He bought a new pear of jeans.

Pick the Homophones

Homophones are words that sound alike, but have different meanings. Look at the homophones in the word bank. Then use them to complete the sentences below.

> whether   by   heal
>
> where   tail   tale   wear
>
> heel   buy   weather

Isabel wants the new book [_____] her favorite author. Her mom promised to [_____] it for her.

I hurt my [_____]. The doctor told me it will take 2 weeks to [_____].

I love parties [_____] people [_____] costumes.

[_____] I go to the gym or jog outside depends on the [_____].

I wrote a [_____] about a dragon with a long, green [_____].

#

These three words sound the same but they all have different meanings!
- Buy is a verb. *You can buy a ticket at the counter.*
- By is a preposition. *I saw a squirrel by the tree.*
- Bye is short for "goodbye".

Complete each sentence with the correct homophone: buy, by, or bye.

Where did you _____ your dress? It's very cute!

_____ the way, have you tried the new frozen yogurt?

I like to _____ popcorn at the zoo.

She knows the song _____ heart.

Do you see the girl sitting _____ Tommy?

_____ ! See you again soon.

I watched the train pass _____ .

I want to _____ a new camera.

It's and its sound the same, but they have different meanings!
- Its is a possessive pronoun. *The dog plays with its tail.*
- It's is a contraction meaning "It is".

Complete the sentences with the correct homophone: it's or its.

The bird picked up a worm with [＿＿＿] beak.

[＿＿＿] time for dinner!

My mom thinks [＿＿＿] good to learn how to swim.

A crocodile uses [＿＿＿] long tail for swimming.

I want to play in the snow, but [＿＿＿] too cold.

The dolphin uses [＿＿＿] fin to control [＿＿＿] direction.

Who's Or Whose

Who's and whose sound the same, but they have different meanings!
- Whose is a possessive pronoun *Whose dog is it?*
- Who's is a contraction meaning "who is."

Complete the sentences with the correct homophone: who's or whose.

[   ] car is parked in the driveway?

I know the kid [   ] bike is red.

Aunt Marie is a person [   ] kind and cheerful.

[   ] shoes are in the hallway?

I think I know [   ] making that squeaky sound.

This party is awesome! [   ] idea was it?

Tommy is a boy [   ] dog can play cool tricks.

Your Or You're

Your and you're sound the same, but they have different meanings!
- Your is a possessive pronoun *Your sister is pretty.*
- You're is a contraction meaning "you are."

Complete the sentence with the correct homophone: your or you're.

Getting lots of sleep is good for [ ] health.

[ ] house is across the street from mine.

Don't forget to bring [ ] lunch box to school.

If [ ] feeling sick, you should go to bed.

When [ ] sad, you want to cry.

[ ] happy because it's your birthday.

The sign says "Please clean up after [ ] meal."

Wow! [ ] wearing [ ] diamond ring.

Their Or They're

These two words sound the same, but they have different meanings!
- Their is a possessive adjective (*Their house is red*).
- They're is a short form of "They are."

Choose the correct word and write it in the blank space to complete the sentence.

The graduates received _____ diplomas.

These toads are jumping high because _____ happy.

The married couple put _____ pictures on the wall.

The chicks always follow _____ mother.

I love the puppies because _____ small and fluffy.

The twins are not allow to drive the car because _____ too young.

I love to eat at Sushi House because _____ food is yummy!

60

A Brief History of the Hula Hoop

Look at the timeline below and answer the questions.

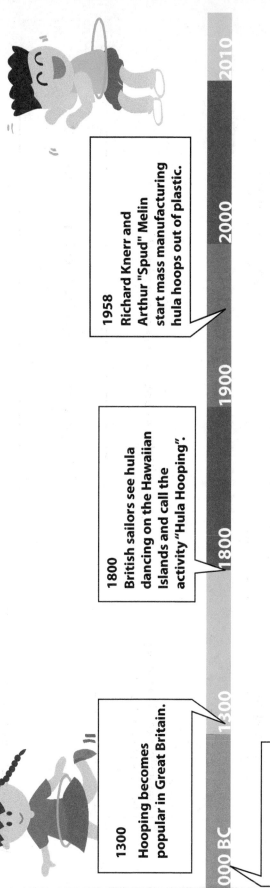

1000 BC
Greeks make hoops out of grape leaves.

1300
Hooping becomes popular in Great Britain.

1800
British sailors see hula dancing on the Hawaiian Islands and call the activity "Hula Hooping".

1958
Richard Knerr and Arthur "Spud" Melin start mass manufacturing hula hoops out of plastic.

1000 BC   1300   1800   1900   2000   2010

In 1000 BC, what material did Greeks use to make hoops?
_____

What happened in Great Britain in 1300?
_____

Where did British sailors see hula dancing?
_____

What did Richard Knerr and Arthur "Spud" Melin do?
_____

A Brief History of Bubble Gum

Look at the timeline below and answer the questions.

1914
William Wrigley, Jr. and Henry Fleer added mint and fruit extracts to chewing gum.

1928
Walter Diemer discovered the perfect bubble gum recipe during his experiment.

1906
Frank Fleer tried to make bubble gum but it was very sticky.

1945
The brand name "Bazooka Bubble gum" was created by The Topps Candy Company.

1900   1910   1920   1930   1940   1950

Whose bubble gum was too sticky?

_____

In what year was the perfect bubble gum discovered?

_____

Who discovered the perfect bubble gum?

_____

What brand of bubble gum was created in 1945?

_____

Synonym Match!

Match each word to its **synonym**.

Synonyms are words that have the same or almost the same meaning.

big	speedy
pretty	little
happy	large
small	damp
fast	begin
start	glad
also	beautiful
wet	too

Plural Practice 1

Draw a line to match the picture to the correct spelling of the singular or plural form.

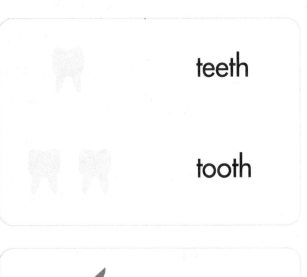

teeth

tooth

women

woman

knives

knife

mouse

mice

person

people

leaves

leaf

Plural Practice 2

Draw a line to match the picture to the correct spelling of the singular or plural form.

child

children

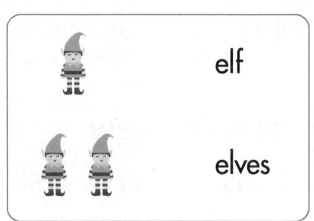

elf

elves

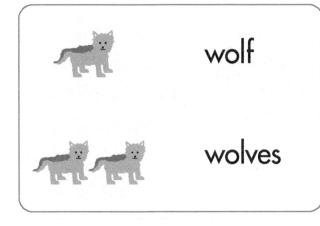

wolf

wolves

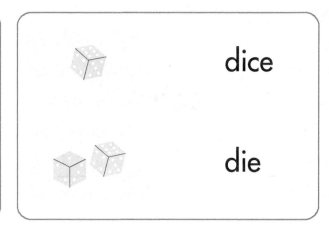

dice

die

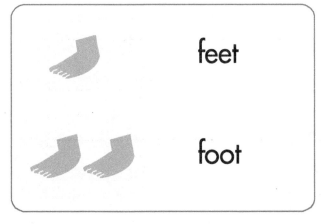

feet

foot

goose

geese

65

Words Ending in Y

All of the words in the word box end in **y**.
If the y word has a **long e** sound, like **baby**,
write the word under the baby.
If the y word has a **long i** sound, like **spy**,
write the word under the spy.

bunny   very   my   sky   happy

fly   cry   shiny   penny   shy

baby

spy

_____

_____

_____

_____

_____

_____

_____

_____

Shh ... Silent Letters

All of these words have silent letters.
Say and rewrite each word. Circle the silent letter or letters.

knee _____

sigh _____

write _____

climb _____

thumb _____

high _____

lamb _____

Silent Letters Crossword

Use the clues to complete the crossword.
All of the answers are words with silent letters.

Across

1. I am a stop _____.

3. I can help you untangle your hair.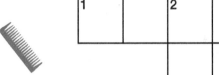

6. I can help you cut your vegetables.

7. I can be difficult to untie.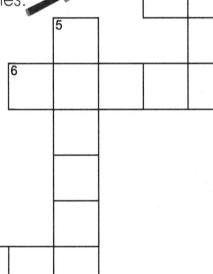

Down

2. I live in a garden and wear a pointed hat.

4. I can explode!

5. I carry a sword and live in a castle.

LET'S GO CAMPING! VOCABULARY

Camping is a fun outdoor activity that provides a chance to explore nature, go hiking, eat over a campfire, stargaze, and sleep in a tent. Watch out for bears as you search for the camping words below! They're spelled forwards, and up and down.

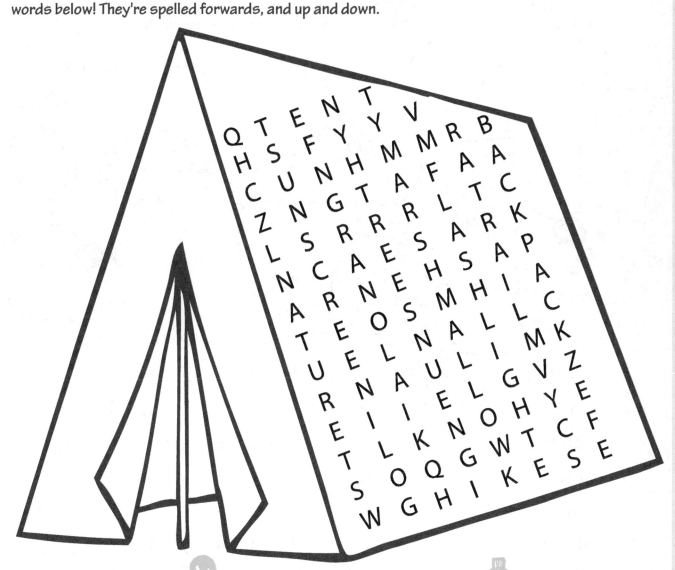

 tent

nature

 sunscreen

backpack

hike

trees

log

flashlight

trail

marshmallow

granola

★ What is your favorite camping activity?

Down on the Farm

Find the names of your favorite things that you can find on a farm in the word search below. They may be written forward, backward, horizontally, vertically, or even diagonally!

When you are done with your word search, color the farm animals!

chicken
cow
farm
dirt
hill
horse
pig
sheep
sun
tree

l	o	k	d	s	m	r	a	f	g
a	d	f	s	u	n	h	j	c	k
d	i	z	x	c	v	b	h	m	l
w	r	c	t	u	y	i	o	r	g
q	t	a	r	s	c	d	r	f	i
z	n	l	e	k	j	h	s	g	p
x	d	c	e	v	b	n	e	m	l
u	b	n	j	g	h	x	w	o	c
o	e	a	u	p	e	e	h	s	i
h	i	l	l	w	a	g	j	p	x

Find the Plural!

Write the plural for each word by adding s or es.
Circle the plural forms in the word search.

A	P	E	N	S	A	N	H
D	Y	E	T	G	L	B	I
B	U	S	E	S	A	O	C
O	S	N	F	X	K	A	D
X	B	C	A	T	S	T	V
E	P	L	O	C	A	S	E
S	G	L	A	S	S	E	S
A	H	E	B	I	J	D	W

cat _____

box _____

boat _____

glass _____

bus _____

pen _____

71

WORDPLAY PUZZLER 1

Look at each list of 3 words. They might not seem to belong in the
same set or category, but don't let the pictures fool you!
Find the one word that ties them all together.
For example, **hair**, **paint** and **tooth** all describe a kind of **brush**.
(hairbrush, paintbrush and toothbrush.)

hair	example		foot	4.
paint	**brush**		beach	
tooth			basket	

pan	1.		book	5.
cheese			earth	
cup			inch	

butter	2.		clown	6.
house			cat	
fire			shell	

tree	3.		sun	7.
club			bird	
bird			bubble	

WORDPLAY PUZZLER 2

Look at each list of 3 words. They might not seem to belong in the
same set or category, but don't let the pictures fool you!
Find the one word that ties them all together.
For example, **hair**, **paint** and **tooth** all describe a kind of **brush**.
(hairbrush, paintbrush, and toothbrush.)

		example
	hair	
	paint	**brush**
	tooth	

		4.
	lip	
	walking	
	drum	

		1.
	note	
	cook	
	phone	

		5.
	baseball	
	bottle	
	skull	

		2.
	head	
	sun	
	night	

		6.
	onion	
	ear	
	diamond	

		3.
	flower	
	river	
	feather	

		7.
	stair	
	suit	
	book	

Great job!

is an Education.com reading superstar

Stu-pen-dous Syllables

Syllables

A syllable is a word or part of a word that is one beat long.
The word **but** has 1 syllable, **butter** has 2 syllables,
and **butterfly** has 3 syllables.

Read each word out loud, and count the syllables.
Write each word on the correct list.

tomorrow   syllable   cat   hamster   also   tonight   sing

done   mittens   monster   important   company

1	2	3
		tomorrow

Fill in the chart by splitting the words into syllables.

	1	2	3
goldfish	gold	fish	
rainstorm			
spaceship			
classroom			
haircut			
newspaper			
skyscraper			

Syllables

A syllable is a word or part of a word that is one beat long.
Read each word out loud, while clapping for each syllable.
Circle the number of syllables for each word.

bones

1 2 3

elephant

1 2 3

net

1 2 3

flowers

1 2 3

baby

1 2 3

banana

1 2 3

Syllables

A syllable is a word or part of a word that is one beat long.
Read each word out loud, while clapping for each syllable.
Circle the number of syllables for each word.

duckling

1 (2) 3 4

mouse

1 2 3 4

crocodile

1 2 3 4

walrus

1 2 3 4

dinosaur

1 2 3 4

butterfly

1 2 3 4

Syllables

Color by Syllables!

Read the words in the picture out loud and count the syllables.
Color the snake according to the color chart.

1 Syllable - Yellow

2 Syllables - Red

3 Syllables - Orange

slithering

viper   jaws

scales

reptile   cobra   fang

poisonous   rattle

snake

venom

Syllables

Color by Syllables!

Read the words in the picture and count the syllables.
Color the bird according to the color chart.

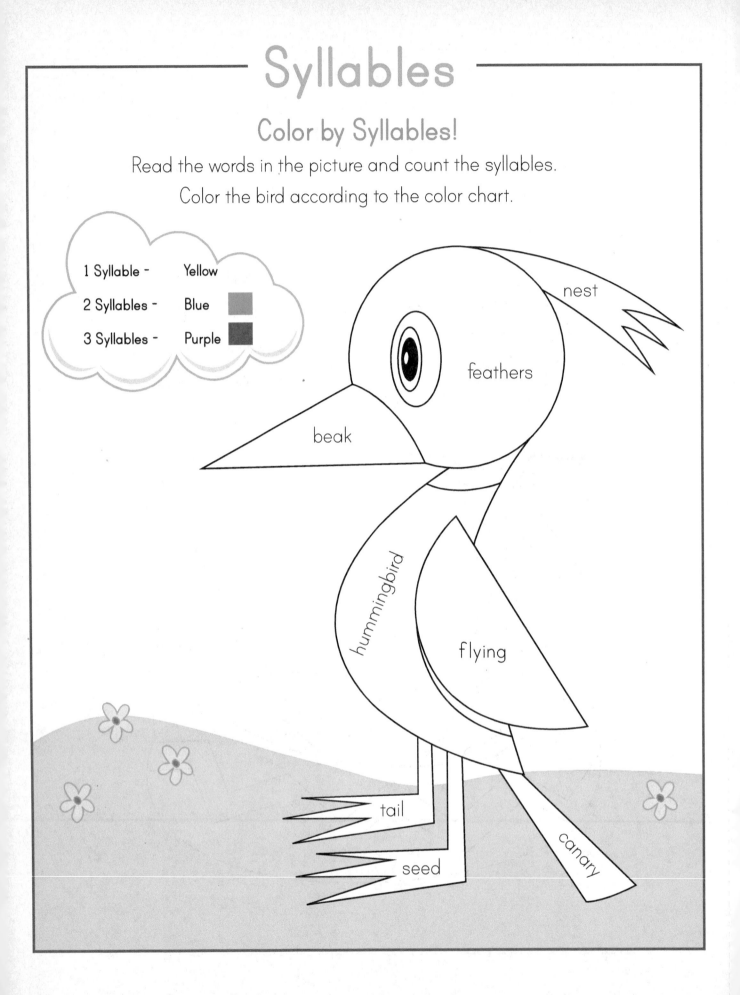

1 Syllable - Yellow

2 Syllables - Blue

3 Syllables - Purple

nest

feathers

beak

hummingbird

flying

tail

seed

canary

Syllables

With the VCV pattern (vowel, consonant, vowel),
a consonant between two vowels sticks with the second vowel.
Write down the number of syllables and draw a slash between the syllables.
HINT: Each syllable has one vowel sound. Divide the syllables BEFORE consonants.

_2_ fi/ner   _____ respect

_____ teacher   _____ trophy

_____ protect   _____ moment

_____ silent   _____ music

Read each three syllable word out loud. Finish dividing each word into syllables.
HINT: Divide the syllables BEFORE consonants

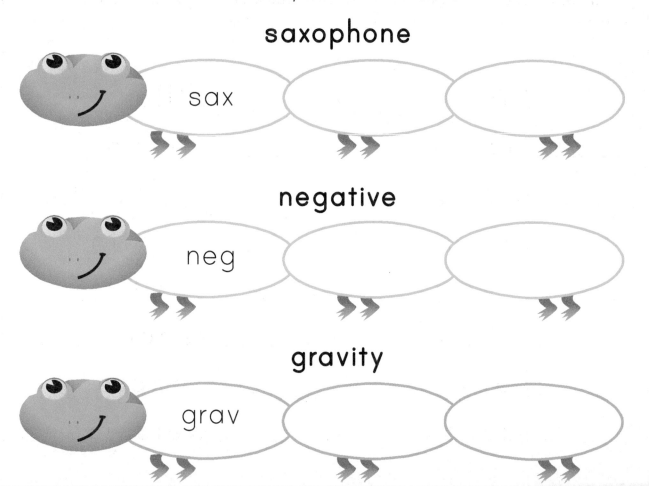

saxophone

sax

negative

neg

gravity

grav

Syllables

Words that follow the VCCV pattern.

Think of VCCV words as a peanut butter and jelly sandwich. The peanut butter and jelly are the consonants, and the slices of bread are the vowels. So, when you split up the word into syllables, the consonants always stick to the vowels!

r a b / b i t

Read each word out loud, counting the syllables.
Write down the number of syllables and draw a slash between the syllables.
HINT: Each syllable has one vowel sound. Divide the syllables BE   TWEEN consonants.

_2_ fun/ny

_____ mattress

_____ pretty

_____ parrot

_____ mirror

_____ giggle

_____ happen

_____ raccoon

_____ pillar

_____ tissue

_____ husband

_____ certain

_____ until

_____ rescue

_____ chapter

_____ welcome

Syllables

With VCCV words, each syllable has one vowel sound.
Syllables are divided between consonants.

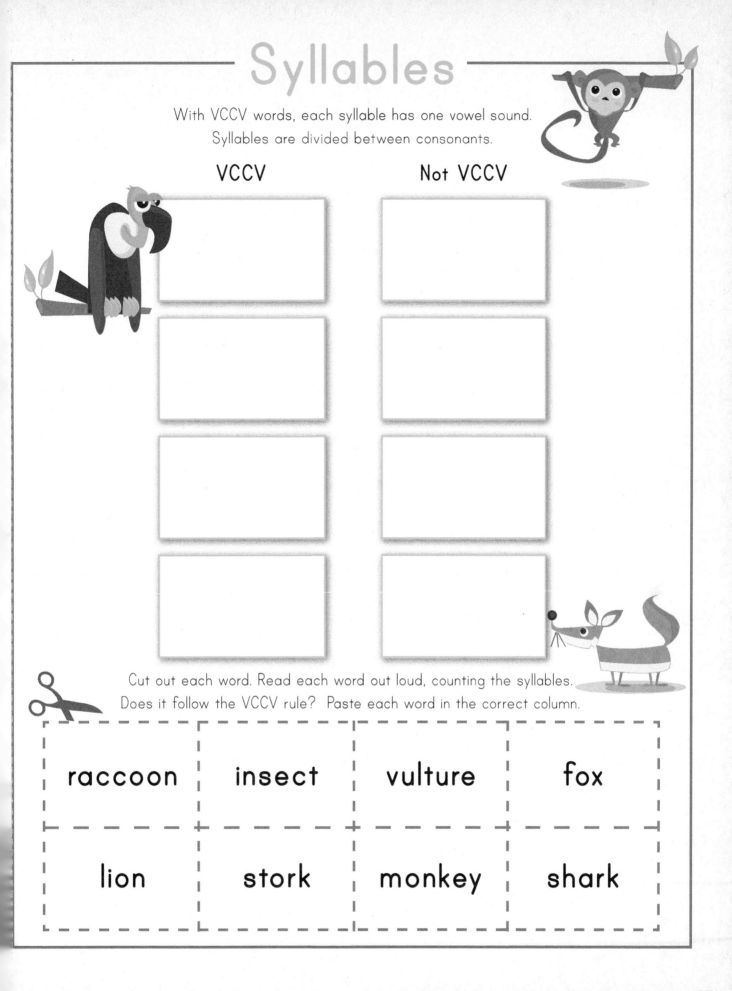

VCCV	Not VCCV

Cut out each word. Read each word out loud, counting the syllables.
Does it follow the VCCV rule? Paste each word in the correct column.

raccoon	insect	vulture	fox
lion	stork	monkey	shark

Syllables

A "Silent-E" syllable ends in an E, has one consonant before the E, and one vowel before the consonant. The pattern is: VCE.

Silent E	Not Silent E

Cut out the name of each word. Read each word out loud. Paste each word in the correct column below.   HINT: Word must end with: Vowel, Consonant, E

whale	little	ice	dye
able	tune	horse	hare

Syllables

With "Consonant-LE" syllables, a consonant is followed by "LE".
The "LE" makes the last syllable.

Consonant LE

Not Consonant LE

Cut out the name of each word. Read each word out loud. Paste each word in
the correct column below.   HINT: A consonant must be before the LE.

| turtle | bubble | puzzle | peephole |
| kale | apple | parole | sale |

Syllables

Read the word out loud, and clap your hands for each syllable. Circle clapping hands for each syllable.

	1	2	3	4
baseball	👏	👏	👏	👏
catch	👏	👏	👏	👏
umpire	👏	👏	👏	👏
infielder	👏	👏	👏	👏
inning	👏	👏	👏	👏
championship	👏	👏	👏	👏
throw	👏	👏	👏	👏
doubleheader	👏	👏	👏	👏

Syllables

VCV and VCCV Syllable Pattern Review

**Count syllables then draw a slash
between the syllables.**

VCV pattern (vowel, consonant, vowel).
Divide the syllables before consonants.

_2_ tro/phy   _____ teacher

_____ because   _____ student

_____ either   _____ chosen

_____ believe   _____ acre

_____ enough   _____ rider

VCCV pattern (vowel, consonant, consonant vowel).
The consonants always stick to the vowels.

_2_ quar/rel   _____ essay

_____ raccoon   _____ announce

_____ cellar   _____ athlete

_____ gossip   _____ husband

_____ appeal   _____ costume

_____ mattress   _____ welcome

_____ terrace   _____ consume

Syllables

Syllables in Animals

A syllable is a word or part of a word that is one beat long.
For example, "cat" has one syllable. "Monkey" has two syllables,
and "elephant" has three syllables.

Practice counting syllables in the names of different kinds of animals

Write in the names of 5 animals. Read each name out loud,
clapping as you count each syllable.

Name	Syllable 1	Syllable 2	Syllable 3	How many?
elephant	el	e	phant	3

Write the name of your pet (or a pet you know): _____

How many syllables are there? _____

Write the name of a cartoon animal: _____

How many syllables are there? _____

Syllables
Read long words!

Did you know you can read, write, and understand longer words
if you break them down into syllables?

Write each syllable in a separate box. Then read the word out loud!

caterpillar	cat	er	pil	lar
difference				
snowmobile				
dishwasher				
emergency				
interesting				
porcupine				
thermometer				
bumblebee				
punctuation				
disappointed				
grandmother				

Syllables
In a Haiku

A haiku is a Japanese poem that is often about nature and the seasons.
Haikus always have three lines, and a specific syllable count.
Read each haiku, and write how many syllables are in each line.

Summer has faded ____5____

Leaves falling, gold and crimson _____

Autumn has begun _____

As the wind does blow _____

Across the trees, I see the _____

Buds blooming in May _____

Whiteness all around _____

Wind and cold and sun abound _____

Who would end this joy? _____

Now write your own haiku, and draw a picture to go with it!

1. _____

2. _____

3. _____

Great job!

is an Education.com reading superstar

Phonics Fun: Vowels and Diphthongs

Just Add E

Add an e to the end of these short vowel words to make new long vowel words.

tub → tub___

can → can___

pin → pin ___

rob → rob___

cub → cub___

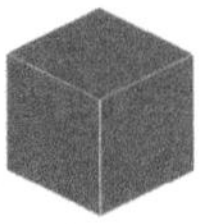

kit → kit ___

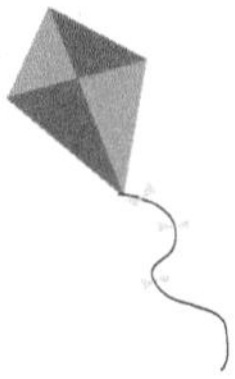

tap → tap ___

man → man___

AUTO Diphthongs

A diphthong is a pair of vowels that make a sound.
"AU" makes the sound in "AUTO."

Finish the sentences with one of the words below.

sauce   taught   autumn   fault

_____ always arrives before winter.

We were _____ the ABC's in kindergarten.

I like tomato _____ on my spaghetti.

It wasn't my _____ that the glass broke.

Find and circle the words with the AU sound.

Because
Caught
Audio
Daughter
Faucet
Vault
Auction
Taut

```
C U I D F I E A F E C V
E D T U T G C U A A T R
C G U L A T T U U A G A
C A C I R N T T C U C U
G I O A T A U O E C C D
A E A T A C A U T T A I
T A U T T U T S E I U O
D A U G H T E R U O G E
U C A H B A D T U N H C
V A U L T H L G B T T I
B E C A U S E A A T H A
T T A N D T G I C U I S
```

The words could
be horizontal
or vertical.

BOIL Diphthongs

A diphthong is a pair of vowels that make a sound.
"OI" makes the sound in "BOIL."

Finish the sentences with one of the words below.

join   spoil   soil   voice

The scary witch had a screechy _____ .

I planted the watermelon seeds in the _____ .

I would like to _____ the Boy Scouts.

If you leave the milk out, it will _____ .

Find and circle the words with the OI sound.

Coin
Oil
Point
Coil
Choice
Toil
Rejoice
Foil

```
R E J O I C E O I L O I
T I L O I I O C I I C L
I R T O O C O I L O H I
I I F O I L L I C F O R
I L O T L I C O O C I H
T L L I O P H O P O C N
O I E E J T R I I I E I
N J L P T L C C P I O F
T N J P L O T T O O E E
I E E C C C I O I I N P
T O I L L I P N N I C O
C O I N O C O I T O O C
```

The words could
be horizontal
or vertical.

CLOUD Diphthongs

A diphthong is a pair of vowels that make a sound.
"OU" makes the sound in "CLOUD."

Finish the sentences with one of the words below.

pound   loud   mountain   mouth

The dentist said, "Open your _____."

We got our new dog from the _____.

I love to hike on the _____.

Turn down the music! It's too _____.

Find and circle the words with the OU sound.
Some words may appear more than once.

About
Out
Sound
Our
Around
House
Found
South

```
U S D A O D S D A S N N
O U U B N U F H U N E D
O D O D A E U H O U S E
U H B O S O S D U U T H
U U T T H A A B O U T F
S D U O S O U T H N U O
O T O U U O T O F N F U
H A O T O O O R H U N N
A R O U N D O U T S E D
S T N H U O U T U H A D
O U U O H U O D D A B O
O U R F O T S O U N D D
```

The words could
be horizontal
or vertical.

123 COUNT Diphthongs

A diphthong is a pair of vowels that make a sound.
"OU" can make the sound in "COUNT."

Finish the sentences with one of the words below.

blouse   ground   bouncy   shout

My mom said, "Don't _____. I can hear you."

For my birthday, I got a red _____ ball.

I spilled juice all over my new _____.

During recess, I tripped and fell to the _____.

**Find and circle the words with the OU sound.
Some words may appear more than once.**

Round
Foul
Nouns
Thousand
Sour
Outside
Abound
Couch

The words could
be horizontal
or vertical.

```
O O E O O O E E A S F S
O D O N O O F N I H O L
O O A H O H N U T D U S
D O H A U U N C H R L S
U D O O A U O O O O A S
U O N S U R U U U U F N
U I O A U L N C S N O R
H E H H O O S H A D E A
O U T S I D E U N U O N
D U U T N O U C D H N R
U S O U R S S O U R T E
C E U A B O U N D O N N
```

104

SAW Diphthongs

A diphthong is a pair of vowels that make a sound.
"AW" makes the sound in "SAW."

Finish the sentences with one of the words below.

lawn   yawn   hawk   crawl

The baby just learned to _____ .

We watched a _____ circle in the sky.

To get allowance, I have to mow the _____ .

During math class, I try not to _____ .

Find and circle the words with the AW sound.

Draw
Straw
Dawn
Slaw
Pawn
Law
Claw
Fawn

```
W A W W L W F F R A A S
A N D R A W C A L S W W
W R L W L L W A W L W A
S A W L N C W N C A C A
A D A T F D W N A W A P
W W F W A A A P W W A A
A N P A W N L W W R N R
A W A N W L A W A A W P
P P W D P F A W N A R N
C L A W W N R A D A W N
A S A A R A C F N N A W
W F W S T R A W W A W A
```

The words could
be horizontal
or vertical.

JEWEL Diphthongs

A diphthong is a pair of vowels that make a sound.
"EW" makes the sound in "JEWEL."

Finish the sentences with one of the words below.

knew   flew   blew   dew

The wind _____ hard during the storm.

Vampire bats _____ during the dark night.

I studied for the test, so I _____ the answers.

In the morning, the grass was wet with _____.

Find and circle the words with the EW sound.

Brew

New

Chew

Drew

Grew

Stew

Renew

Threw

```
G H R H W R W E R T W T
R W W W N W B R R H E E
E E W E N R R D E R R S
W R W E E W E R E E E W
R N E E H N W E S W E S
E R E H G E R W N E E T
G N R W W C E D W C H E
T H T R E H N W R E W W
E E T T W E E W W W R W
E W G H E W E W W W E T N
R E N E W W N E W E N E
R G N W T N W R C S W H
```

The words could
be horizontal
or vertical.

OWL Diphthongs

A diphthong is a combination of letters
that makes a complex vowel sound.

"OW" makes the sound in "OWL."

Finish the sentences with one of the words below.

cows   clown   meow   flowers

I like to pick _____ in the garden.

Our new little kitten said _____ !

A funny _____ performed at the circus.

Black and white _____ grazed in the field.

Find and circle the words with the OW sound.

Power
Drown
Wow
Town
Plow
Brown
Growl
Vowel

```
D R O W N O O V W G L O
G N N T O E V R L N R W
W P W W B N W W N N O B
L O R R W R O T O R V L
O O P N D W B O W T O W
R O O W N O R R E R W L
L E W W O P L O W W E E
N W O V W D O N O W L O
B R O W N G R O W L T W
O W O W W W T D L W O O
R W G P O W E R W D W N
R L W O W N G B T L N W
```

The words could
be horizontal
or vertical.

TOY Diphthongs

A diphthong is a pair of vowels that make a sound.
"OY" makes the sound in "TOY."

Finish the sentences with one of the words below.

joyful   royal   enjoy   loyal

The queen led the _____ parade.

Christmas is a _____ holiday!

I _____ sleeping in late on Saturdays.

My dog is a _____ friend to me.

Find and circle the words with the OY sound.
Some words may appear more than once.

Boy
Joy
Soy
Decoy
Cowboy
Toy
Ahoy
Annoy

```
D O B H Y O Y N N S Y W
E O A S B Y Y H D O O O
C N T H W B N Y O C Y Y
O N O A Y O O O T O A J
Y B A J C O W B O Y S B
T Y C O O Y O O Y Y O O
O A H O Y B O Y N O Y Y
Y O O E O S B C N O T B
Y O N Y J Y E O Y Y J N
C O N C Y O B A Y B A H
S A A N N O Y N C T B Y
J O Y Y B Y Y J Y C Y W
```

The words could
be horizontal
or vertical.

Great job!

is an Education.com reading superstar

SPELLING PATTERNS: ENDINGS

How to Make a Noun Plural page 4

witch —— witches

airplane —— airplanes

box —— boxes

book —— books

sock —— socks

horse —— horses

lemon —— lemons

More Than One page 5

apple —— apples

fox —— foxes

brush —— brushes

ball —— balls

tent —— tents

sandwich —— sandwiches

watch —— watches

axe —— axes

pig —— pigs

house —— houses

bee —— bees

tomato —— tomatoes

potato —— potatoes

Plurals Word Search page 6

pencil —— pencils

fox —— foxes

house —— houses

witch —— witches

cup —— cups

crayon —— crayons

cat —— cats

box —— boxes

B	O	X	E	S	B	R	Y
C	W	I	T	C	H	E	S
R	I	X	E	S	Q	C	G
A	J	C	U	P	S	A	F
Y	M	U	Z	O	E	T	O
O	O	P	E	S	A	S	X
N	H	O	U	S	E	S	E
S	P	E	N	C	I	L	S

Ends in Y page 7

berry —— berries

baby —— babies

bunny —— bunnies

boy —— boys

key —— keys

fly —— flies

spy —— spies

monkey —— monkeys

tray —— trays

toy —— toys

The Irregular Plural Noun page 8

leaf —— leaves

tooth —— teeth

goose —— geese

scarf —— scarves

kiss —— kisses

wolf —— wolves

More Irregular Plural Nouns page 9

child —— children

person —— people

foot —— feet

ox —— oxen

woman —— women

fish —— fish

Basic Past Tense page 11

1. We **depended** on the car to get from home to school, but now we ride the bus to school.

2. The students **handed** in their homework to the teacher.

3. I **chased** the ball across the field.

4. Yes, I **asked** to go to the park.

5. We **walked** around the lake.

Double the Consonant page 12

stop —— stopped

skip —— skipped

hop —— hopped

sob —— sobbed

Verbs that End in E page 13

smile —— smiled

pick —— picked

pinch —— pinched

sneeze —— sneezed

race —— raced

paint —— painted

rain —— rained

help —— helped

P	A	I	N	T	E	D	S
I	S	M	I	L	E	D	N
N	A	E	D	E	P	R	E
C	T	K	O	Q	D	A	E
H	V	X	C	B	U	I	Z
E	R	A	C	E	D	N	E
D	X	H	E	L	P	E	D
P	I	C	K	E	D	D	J

SPELLING PATTERNS: ENDINGS

Verbs that End in Y   page 14

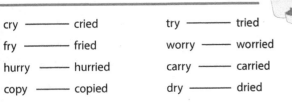

cry ———— cried   try ———— tried

fry ———— fried   worry ———— worried

hurry ——— hurried   carry ——— carried

copy ———— copied   dry ———— dried

B	T	A	R	F	W	C	X
C	R	I	E	D	O	A	H
O	I	A	B	H	R	R	U
P	E	I	S	Q	R	R	R
I	D	P	R	B	I	I	R
E	H	Y	I	P	E	E	I
D	R	I	E	D	D	D	E
F	R	I	E	D	I	E	D

The Sounds ED Can Make   page 15

id	d	t
batted	played	blinked
exited	bloomed	baked
added	agreed	dumped
	loved	talked
	smiled	

Spot the Ending   page 16

wash	wasshed	washd	(washed)
relax	relaxd	(relaxed)	relaxxed
clean	(cleaned)	cleanned	cleand
smile	(smiled)	smild	smiled
visit	visits	(visited)	visitted
invite	invites	invitedd	(invited)
call	calld	caled	(called)
pry	(pried)	pryed	pryedd
live	livd	(lived)	livved
spy	spiedd	spide	(spied)

Verbs with ING   page 17

1. Are you **trying** to open the door?

2. He is **playing** basketball with his friends.

3. She is **baking** a cake for the party.

4. We are **listening** to music.

5. Tim is **riding** his bike to school.

6. Sara is **looking** for a book to read.

7. Our school is **recycling** paper and plastic.

8. I am **feeding** the cat.

Double the Consonant First   page 18

tap ———— tapping   swim ——— swimming

pop ———— popping   sip ———— sipping

Take Away the E   page 19

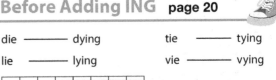

1. I am **dancing** to my favorite song.

2. We are **making** a card for our mom's birthday.

3. We are **baking** brownies!

4. He is **waking** up.

5. Everyone is **smiling** for the class picture.

6. Dad is **taking** us to the zoo right now.

Change IE to Y Before Adding ING   page 20

die ———— dying   tie ———— tying

lie ———— lying   vie ———— vying

I	T	A	V	Y	I	N	G
F	R	T	Y	I	N	G	R
I	D	K	X	R	S	H	E
G	Y	L	H	M	E	R	W
N	I	N	A	Y	G	E	J
T	N	G	D	Z	W	T	U
R	G	A	R	Q	R	R	N
B	A	L	Y	I	N	G	G

SPELLING PATTERNS: ENDINGS

Consonant Endings: ED and ING page 21

walk	walkked	(walked)	(walking)	wakking
jump	(jumped)	jumpped	jumpping	(jumping)
slap	(slapped)	slaping	(slapping)	slaped
pin	(pinned)	(pinning)	pined	pineng
dot	doted	(dotted)	doting	(dotting)
tan	(tanned)	taning	taned	(tanning)
wag	wagdd	(wagged)	waggeng	(wagging)
wink	winkdd	(winked)	(winking)	winkking
tug	tuging	tuged	(tugging)	(tugged)
pull	puling	(pulled)	(pulling)	puled

1. Frank **tapped** his foot to the music.

2. Kristi is **putting** the cake in the oven.

3. Mindy **played** with her friends after school.

4. Mark is **looking** for his other sock.

An End   page 22

wish ——— wished   cry ——— cried

stop ——— stopped   cough ——— coughed

hurry ——— hurried   sneeze ——— sneezed

laugh ——— laughed   pop ——— popped

nod ——— nodded   time ——— timed

1. At the Halloween party we are **bobbing** for apples.

2. He is **worrying** about the math test this week.

3. She is **waving** at the animals at the zoo.

4. They are **keeping** their house clean by sweeping every day.

5. Mike does not like **taking** the trash out.

6. Mom was **smelling** the flowers at the park.

PREFIXES AND SUFFIXES

What is a Prefix? page 26

Night	Candle	Drive	Tour
(Untie)	Lit	(Return)	Run
Order	(Mistake)	Turn	(Reverse)

What is a Suffix? page 27

Pig	Drive	Act	(Careful)
(Piglet)	Teach	(Painless)	Night
Actor	(Darkness)	Care	Untie

Compound Words page 28

jellyfish	jelly	fish
butterflies	butter	flies

Write Comparing Words page 29

warm	warmer	warmest
thick	thicker	thickest
hard	harder	hardest
sweet	sweeter	sweetest
slow	slower	slowest
cold	colder	coldest

Vowel & Consonant Suffixes page 30

1. The cat **begged** for the mouse toy.
2. Aunt Dottie **stopped** at the red light.
3. I enjoy **sitting** by the fire.
4. My firends **popped** the balloon.
5. The Dalmatian is very **spotty**.

Vowel & Consonant Suffixes page 31

1. My sister's room is very tidy and **spotless.**
2. Which is **tastier**, gummy bears or popcorn?
3. Jeremy **shops** at the store for a new tie.
4. I **gladly** ate the candy apples.
5. Gina **slips** the collar over the dog's head.
6. My brother is **sloppier** than I am.
7. I love running and **fitness.**
8. John thinks clowns are the **funniest** people in the world.

Special Suffix Rules page 32

1. **Happiness:**
   a. Write out the suffix: **ness**
   b. Does the word start with a vowel or consonant? **consonant**
   c. Break down the word into syllables: **hap-pi-ness**
2. **Understanding:**
   a. Write out the suffix: **ing**
   b. Does the word start with a vowel or consonant? **vowel**
   c. Break down the work into syllables: **un-der-stand-ing**

Negative Nellie page 34

1. Nellie is a very **un**happy person.
2. She's never pleased and is always **dis**appointed.
3. **Im**patient and quick-tempered, she gets angry easily.
4. Nellie has many **dis**likes and enjoys very little.
5. Nellie is humor**less** and grumpy.
6. She's incredibly **im**polite to teachers and other adults.
7. She is care**less** with toys that don't belong to her.
8. Nellie dislikes many people and is very **anti**social.

PREFIXES AND SUFFIXES

Positive Pete page 35

1. Pete is a very hope**ful** and positive person.

2. His friends say he **over**flows with happiness.

3. He is very **pro**active and always does the best thing.

4. Sometimes Pete is called child**ish**, but he's just playful.

5. Pete is rather clown**ish** and loves to make others laugh.

6. He is very thought**ful** and loves gift-giving.

7. Respect**ful** and sweet, Pete has many good qualities.

More, Most, and Suffixes page 36

1. I find my sister is way **more** cheerful than my brother.

2. Puppies are the **most** playful pets.

3. Do you think elephants or sharks are **more** powerful?

1. Sometimes Joe can be **more** talkative outside of class.

2. Cooks try to find the **most** meal combinations.

3. Are monkeys **more** entertaining than cats?

Testing Suffix Skills page 37

1. My cookie is **bigger** than my brother's, but our father chose the **biggest** cookie from the jar.

2. The dog was **happier** than the cat when you gave him a bone, but he was the **happiest** when we played fetch with him.

3. I thought the kitten was **more playful** than the cat, but the puppy was the **most playful** out of all the animals in the pet store.

4. John **gladly** picked the first ice cream scoop.

5. Which do you find **funnier**, a monkey or a clown?

6. The movie made me **sadder** the more I watched it.

Practice Number Prefixes page 38

bi	+	cycle	=	bicycle
tri	+	angle	=	triangle
uni	+	corn	=	unicorn
tri	+	pod	=	tripod

Make New Words With Suffixes page 39

chew	+	-able	=	chewable
color	+	-ful	=	colorful
treat	+	-less	=	treatless
like	+	-able	=	likable
sad	+	-ly	=	sadly
fair	+	-ness	=	fairness
help	+	-ful	=	helpful
silent	+	-ly	=	silently

** There are many combinations that work for these.

Unscrambling Prefixes page 40

1. eradmim: **mermaid**

2. uaumqari: **aquarium**

3. tusoopc: **octopus**

4. eepeltcos: **telescope**

5. lugasle: **seagull**

6. lozooyg: **zoology**

7. suaienrmb: **submarine**

8. edawnerrut: **underwater**

Prefix Search page 41

An unhappy crow choking with thirst saw a big clay jug, and hoping to find water, flew to it with delight. When he reached it, he sadly realized that it contained so little water that he could not possibly get at it.

He tried everything he could think of to reach the water, but all his efforts were in vain.

Suddenly, the crow had an idea! He flew away and returned with a stone, dropping it into the pitcher. The water raised a little, making room for the stone. Happy with his discovery, the crow collected as many stones as he could carry and dropped them one by one with his beak into the pitcher, until he brought the water within his reach and had a nice, refreshing drink!

Little by little does the trick.

ANSWERS

Suffix Search   page 42

Once when a lion was (sleeping) a little mouse began (running) up and down on top of him; this soon woke up the lion, who (placed) his huge paw on top of him, and (opened) his big jaws to swallow him.

"Pardon, O King," (squeaked) the little mouse: "forgive me this time, I shall never forget it: I promise if you let me go now, I'll pay you back!"

The lion was so (tickled) at the idea of the mouse (helping) him, that he (lifted) up his paw and let him go.

Some time after the lion was stuck in a rope trap (dangling) in the trees. Just then the little mouse (walked) by, and (seeing) how sad the lion was, went up to him and soon (chewed) away the ropes that bound the King of the Beasts, (proving) his worth as a good friend.

Even small friends are great friends.

Prefix/Suffix Multiple Choice   page 46

1. I loved the movie so much I had to **rewatch** it.
　　B. I liked the movie so much I watched it again.

2. I want to be a **writer** when I grow up!
　　C. I want to write for a living when I'm older.

3. My mom **disconnected** the cable from my TV.
　　C. My mom removed the cable from my TV.

4. Sally got to **preview** the book before class.
　　B. Sally got to read the book before class.

5. Mary is a very **helpful** student.
　　C. As a student, Mary helps a lot.

6. John **unwrapped** his present during the party.
　　C. John opened his present during the party.

Build a Wall   page 43

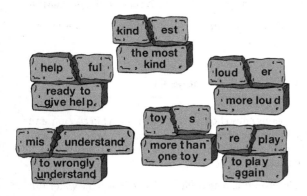

Prefix Crossword Puzzle   page 45

Across:

2. centipede

4. alligator

Down:

1. feline

3. anteater

5. octopus

VOCABULARY IN FOCUS

Same Sounds   page 52

1. I just (eight / (ate)) a lot of ((meat) / meet) for dinner.

2. I can't ((wait) / weight) to receive your letter in the (male / (mail))!

3. My mom bought ((two) / to) pounds of delicious (beats / (beets)).

4. Jack is spending the (weak / (week)) with his ((aunt) / ant).

5. We ((won) / one) (hour / (our)) first basketball game!

6. Would you like to (where / (wear)) a (pear / (pair)) of my mittens?

7. Mr. Smith's ((son) / sun) is an (I / (eye)) doctor.

8. (Their / (There)) is an (acts / (ax)) over by the tree.

Simone's Homophones   page 53

1. I walked **into** the pet store because **there** was a sign that said "Puppies for **Sale**." The cutest one had a short tail and white **paws**.

2. When I'm **bored** and my mom isn't home, I like **to** try on her high **heeled** shoes. **They're** difficult to **wear**, but they make me three inches taller.

3. My cousin Julius **sent** me a postcard in the **mail**. He is at the beach in Hawaii with his **new** surfboard. He has been surfing **for** over twenty years.

4. I can't **wait** for softball season this year. My **two** favorite positions to play are **right** field and third **base**.

Check the Homophones   page 54

1. I didn't (sea) any squirrels at the park.   **see**

2. I can't (weight) for my friend to call back.   **wait**

3. I (cent) Roy a present for his birthday.   **sent**

4. John's (made) washed his clothes.   **maid**

5. Yesterday I (war) my favorite skirt to school.   **wore**

6. Watch out for (bares)!   **bears**

7. He bought a new (pear) of jeans.   **pair**

Pick the Homophones   page 55

1. Isabel wants the new book **by** her favorite author. Her mom promised to **buy** it for her.

2. I hurt my **heel** . The doctor told me it will take 2 weeks to **heal** .

3. I love parties **where** people **wear** costumes.

4. **Whether** I go to the gym or jog outside depends on the **weather**.

5. I wrote a **tale** about a dragon with a long green **tail**.

VOCABULARY IN FOCUS

 **page 56**

1. Where did you **buy** your dress? It's very cute!

2. By the way, have you tried the new frozen yogurt?

3. I like to **buy** popcorn at the zoo.

4. She knows the song **by** heart.

5. Do you see the girl sitting **by** Tommy?

6. Bye! See you again soon.

7. I watched the train pass **by**.

8. I want to **buy** a new camera.

 page 57

1. The bird picked up a worm with **its** beak.

2. It's time for dinner!

3. My mom thinks **it's** good to learn how to swim.

4. A crocodile uses **its** long tail for swimming.

5. I want to play in the snow, but **it's** too cold.

6. The dolphin uses **its** fin to control **its** direction.

 page 58

1. Whose car is parked in the driveway?

2. I know the kid **whose** bike is red.

3. Aunt Marie is a person **who's** kind and cheerful.

4. Whose shoes are in the hallway?

5. I think I know **who's** making that squeaky sound.

6. This party is awesome! **Whose** idea was it?

7. Tommy is a boy **whose** dog can play cool tricks.

Your Or You're **page 59**

1. Getting lots of sleep is good for **your** health.

2. Your house is across the street from mine.

3. Don't forget to bring **your** lunch box to school.

4. If **you're** feeling sick, you should go to bed.

5. When **you're** sad, you want to cry.

6. You're happy because it's your birthday.

7. The sign says "Please clean up after **your** meal."

8. Wow! **You're** wearing **your** diamond ring!

Their Or They're **page 60**

1. The graduates received **their** diplomas.

2. These toads are jumping high because **they're** happy.

3. The married couple put **their** pictures on the wall.

4. The chicks always follow **their** mother.

5. I love puppies because **they're** small and fluffy.

6. The twins are not allowed to drive the car because **they're** too young.

7. I love to eat at Sushi House because **their** food is yummy!

Hula Hoop History **page 61**

1. What did Richard Knerr and Arther "Spud" Melin do?
They started mass manufacturing hula hoops out of plastic.

2. In 1000 BC, what material did Greeks use to make hoops?
Grape leaves.

3. What happened in Great Britain in 1300?
Hooping became popular.

4. Where did British sailors see hula dancing?
On the Hawaiian islands.

VOCABULARY IN FOCUS

Bubble Gum History **page 62**

1. What brand of bubble gum was created in 1945?
Bazooka Bubble Gum.

2. Whose bubble gum was too sticky?
Frank Fleer's

3. In what year was the perfect bubble gum discovered?
1928.

4. Who discovered the perfect bubble gum?
Walter Diemer.

Synonym Match! **page 63**

big ——— large   fast ——— speedy
pretty ——— beautiful   start ——— begin
happy ——— glad   also ——— too
small ——— little   wet ——— damp

Plural Practice 1 **page 64**

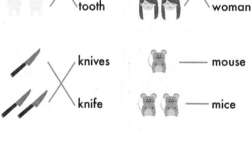

teeth
tooth
women
woman
knives
knife
mouse
mice
person
people
leaves
leaf

Plural Practice 2 **page 65**

child
children
elf
elves

wolf
wolves
dice
die

feet
foot
goose
geese

Words Ending in Y **page 66**

Long E Sound: baby, bunny, very, happy, shiny, penny
Long I Sound: spy, my, sky, fly, cry, shy

Shh ... Silent Letters **page 67**

knee   thumb
sigh   high
write   lamb
climb

Silent Letters Crossword **page 68**

Across: **Down:**
1. Sign   **2.** Gnome
3. Comb   **4.** Bomb
6. Knife   **5.** Knight
7. Knot

VOCABULARY IN FOCUS

LET'S GO CAMPING page 69

```
Q T E N T
H S F Y Y V
C U N H M M R B
Z L N G T A F A A
  N C R R R L T C
  A E A E S A R K
  T R N E H S A P
  U E O S M H I A
  R L N A L L C
  E N A U L I M K
  I I E L G V Z
  L K N O H Y E
  S O Q G W T C F
  W G H I K E S E
```

DOWN ON THE FARM page 70

```
l o k d s m r a f g
a d f s u n h j c k
d i z x c v b h m l
w r c t u y i o r g
q t a r s c d r f i
z n l e k j h s g p
x d c e v b n e m l
u b n j g h x w o c
o e a u p e e h s i
h i l l w a g j p x
```

Find the Plural! page 71

cat——cats   glass——glasses
box——boxes   bus——busses
boat——boats   pen——pens

A	P	E	N	S	A	N	H
D	Y	E	T	G	L	B	I
B	U	S	E	S	A	O	C
O	S	N	F	X	K	A	D
X	B	C	A	T	S	T	V
E	P	L	O	C	A	S	E
S	G	L	A	S	S	E	S
A	H	E	B	I	J	D	W

WORDPLAY PUZZLER 1 page 72

1. Cake   5. Worm
2. Fly   6. Fish
3. House   7. Bath
4. Ball

WORDPLAY PUZZLER 2 page 73

1. Book   5. Cap
2. Light   6. Ring
3. Bed   7. Case
4. Stick

STU-PEN-DOUS SYLLABLES

Syllables page 78

1	2	3
cat	hamster	tomorrow
sing	also	syllable
done	tonight	important
	mittens	company
	monster	

	1	2	3
goldfish	gold	fish	—
rainstorm	rain	storm	—
spaceship	space	ship	—
classroom	class	room	—
haircut	hair	cut	—
newspaper	news	pa	per
skyscraper	sky	scra	per

Syllables page 79

bones	(1)	2	3
elephant	1	2	(3)
net	(1)	2	3
flowers	1	(2)	3
baby	1	(2)	3
banana	1	2	(3)

Syllables page 80

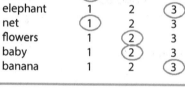

duckling	1	(2)	3
mouse	(1)	2	3
crocodile	1	2	(3)
walrus	1	(2)	3
dinosaur	1	2	(3)
butterfly	1	2	(3)

Syllables (Color by Syllables) page 81

slithering	3 (orange)	fang	1 (yellow)
viper	2 (red)	venom	2 (red)
jaws	1 (yellow)	snake	1 (yellow)
scales	1 (yellow)	rattle	2 (red)
reptile	2 (red)	poisonous	3 (orange)
cobra	2 (red)		

Syllables (Color by Syllables) page 82

nest	1 (yellow)	flying	2 (blue)
feathers	2 (blue)	tail	1 (yellow)
beak	1 (yellow)	seed	1 (yellow)
hummingbird	3 (purple)	canary	3 (purple)

Syllables (VCV Patterns) page 83

fi/ner	= 2	re/spect	= 2
tea/cher	= 2	tro/phy	= 2
pro/tect	= 2	mo/ment	= 2
si/lent	= 2	mu/sic	= 2

saxophone = sax/o/phone
negative = neg/a/tive
gravity = grav/i/ty

Syllables (VCCV Patterns) page 84

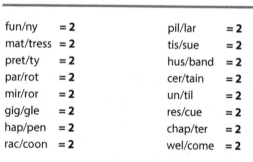

fun/ny	= 2	pil/lar	= 2
mat/tress	= 2	tis/sue	= 2
pret/ty	= 2	hus/band	= 2
par/rot	= 2	cer/tain	= 2
mir/ror	= 2	un/til	= 2
gig/gle	= 2	res/cue	= 2
hap/pen	= 2	chap/ter	= 2
rac/coon	= 2	wel/come	= 2

Syllables (VCCV Patterns) page 85

VCCV: raccoon, insect, vulture, monkey
Not VCCV: fox, lion, stork, shark

STU-PEN-DOUS SYLLABLES

ANSWERS

Syllables (Silent E) **page 87**

Silent E: whale, ice, tune, hare
Not Silent E: little, dye, able, horse

Syllables (Consonant-LE) **page 89**

Consonant-LE: turtle, bubble, puzzle, apple
Not Consonant-LE: peephole, kale, parole, sale

Syllables (Clapping Baseball) **page 91**

base/ball	= 2	in/ning	= 2
catch	= 1	cham/pi/on/ship	= 4
um/pire	= 2	throw	= 1
in/fiel/der	= 3	dou/ble/hea/der	= 4

Syllables (VCV and VCCV Review)

VCV Pattern		VCCV Pattern			
tro/phy	= 2	quar/rel	= 2	hus/band	= 2
be/cause	= 2	rac/coon	= 2	cos/tume	= 2
ei/ther	= 2	cel/lar	= 2	wel/come	= 2
be/lieve	= 2	gos/sip	= 2	con/sume	= 2
e/nough	= 2	ap/peal	= 2		
tea/cher	= 2	mat/tress	= 2		
stu/dent	= 2	ter/race	= 2		
cho/sen	= 2	es/say	= 2		
a/cre	= 2	an/nouce	= 2		
ri/der	= 2	ath/lete	= 2		

page 92

Syllables (Read Long Words) **page 94**

	1	2	3	4
caterpillar	cat	er	pil	lar
difference	dif	fer	ence	—
snowmobile	snow	mo	bile	—
dishwasher	dish	wash	er	—
emergency	e	mer	gen	cy
interesting	in	ter	est	ing
porcupine	por	cu	pine	—
thermometer	ther	mom	e	ter
bumblebee	bum	ble	bee	—
punctuation	punc	tu	a	tion
disappointed	dis	ap	point	ed
grandmother	grand	moth	er	—

Syllables (Haiku) **page 95**

5	Sum/mer has fad/ed
7	Leaves fal/ling, gold and crim/son
5	Au/tumn has be/gun
5	As the wind does blow
7	A/cross the trees, I see the
5	Buds bloom/ing in May
5	White/ness all a/round
7	Wind and cold and sun a/bound
5	Who would end this joy?

PHONICS FUN

Just Add E page 100

tub ——— tube

cub ——— cube

can ——— cane

kit ——— kite

pin ——— pine

tap ——— tape

rob ——— robe

man ——— mane

AUTO Diphthongs page 101

1. **Autumn** always arrives before winter.

2. We were **taught** the ABC's in kindergarten.

3. I like tomato **sauce** on my spaghetti.

4. It wasn't my **fault** that the glass broke.

```
C U I D F I E A F E C V
E D T U T G C U A A T R
C G U L A T T U U A G A
C A C I R N T T C U C U
G I O A T A U O E C C D
A E A T A C A U T T A I
T A U T T U T S E I U O
D A U G H T E R U O G E
U C A H B A D T U N H C
V A U L T H L G B T T I
B E C A U S E A A T H A
T T A N D T G I C U I S
```

BOIL Diphthongs page 102

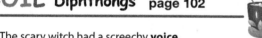

1. The scary witch had a screechy **voice.**

2. I planted the watermelon seeds in the **soil.**

3. I would like to **join** the Boy Scouts.

4. If you leave milk out, it will **spoil.**

```
R E J O I C E O I L O I
T I L O I I O C I I C L
I R T O O C O I L O H I
I I F O I L L I C F O R
I L O T L I C O O C I H
T L L I O P H O P O C N
O I E E J T R I I I E I
N J L P T L C C P I O F
T N J P L O T T O O E E
I E E C C C I O I I N P
T O I L L I P N N I C O
C O I N O C O I T O O C
```

CLOUD Diphthongs page 103

1. The dentist said, "Open your **mouth.**"

2. We got our new dog from the **pound.**

3. I love to hike on the **mountain.**

4. Turn down the music! It's too **loud.**

```
U S D A O D S D A S N N
O U U B N U F H U N E D
O D O D A E U H O U S E
U H B O S O S D U U T H
U U T T H A A B O U T F
S D U O S O U T H N U O
O T O U U O T O F N F U
H A O T O O O R H U N N
A R O U N D O U T S E D
S T N H U O U T U H A D
O U U O H U O D D A B O
O U R F O T S O U N D D
```

COUNT Diphthongs page 104

1. My mom said, "Don't **shout.** I can hear you."

2. For my birthday, I got a red **bouncy** ball.

3. I spilled juice all over my new **blouse.**

4. During recess, I tripped and fell to the **ground.**

```
O O E O O O O E E A S F S
O D O N O O F N I H O L
O O A H O H N U T D U S
D O H A U U N C H R L S
U D O O A U O O O O A S
U O N S U R U U U U F N
U I O A U L N C S N O R
H E H H O O S H A D E A
O U T S I D E U N U O N
D U U T N O U C D H N R
U S O U R S S O U R T E
C E U A B O U N D O N N
```

123

PHONICS FUN

SAW Diphthongs   page 105

1. The baby just learned to **crawl.**

2. We watched a **hawk** circle in the sky.

3. To get allowance, I have to mow the **lawn.**

4. During my math class, I try not to **yawn.**

```
W A W W L W F F R A A S
A N D R A W C A L S W W
W R L W L L W A W L W A
S A W L N C W N C A C A
A D A T F D W N A W A P
W W F W A A A P W W A A
A N P A W N L W W R N R
A W A N W L A W A A W P
P P W D P F A W N A R N
C L A W W N R A D A W N
A S A A R A C F N N A W
W F W S T R A W W A W A
```

OWL Diphthongs   page 107

1. I like to pick **flowers** in the garden.

2. Our new little kitten said **meow!**

3. A funny **clown** performed at the circus.

4. Black and white **cows** grazed in the field.

```
D R O W N O O V W G L O
G N N T O E V R L N R W
W P W W B N W W N N O B
L O R R W R O T O R V L
O O P N D W B O W T O W
R O O W N O R R E R W L
L E W W O P L O W W E E
N W O V W D O N O W L O
B R O W N G R O W L T W
O W O W W W T D L W O O
R W G P O W E R W D W N
R L W O W N G B T L N W
```

JEWEL Diphthongs   page 106

1. The wind **blew** hard during the storm.

2. Vampire bats **flew** during the dark night.

3. I studied for the test, so I **knew** the answers.

4. In the morning, the grass was wet with **dew.**

```
G H R H W R W E R T W T
R W W W N W B R R H E E
E E W E N R R D E R R S
W R W E E W E R E E E W
R N E E H N W E S W E S
E R E H G E R W N E E T
G N R W W C E D W C H E
T H T R E H N W R E W W
E E T T W E E W W W R W
E W G H E W E W W E T N
R E N E W W N E W E N E
R G N W T N W R C S W H
```

TOY Diphthongs   page 108

1. The queen led the **royal** parade.

2. Christmas is a **joyful** holiday!

3. I **enjoy** sleeping in late on Saturday.

4. My dog is a **loyal** friend to me.

```
D O B H Y O Y N N S Y W
E O A S B Y Y H D O O O
C N T H W B N Y O C Y Y
O N O A Y O O O T O A J
Y B A J C O W B O Y S B
T Y C O O Y O O Y Y O O
O A H O Y B O Y N O Y Y
Y O O E O S B C N O T B
Y O N Y J Y E O Y Y J N
C O N C Y O B A Y B A H
S A A N N O Y N C T B Y
J O Y Y B Y Y J Y C Y W
```